Contents

What is a mythical creature?

Stories around the world tell us about strange creatures, such as werewolves and fairies. For many years people have wondered if these **mythical** creatures really exist. What do you think?

DID YOU KNOW?
People tell vampire stories in Europe, Africa, Asia, Australia, and South America.

Have you heard stories about mermaids? Do you think they could exist?

What is a dragon?

Myths from around the world tell us about dragons. These huge monsters are shown in many paintings. They often look like giant lizards or crocodiles.

DID YOU KNOW?

The Thai Dragon is a very hot chilli pepper used in Asian cooking. When people eat the pepper it feels as if they are breathing fire!

The dragons in many stories breathe
fire. Other dragons fly high in the air.
Some **myths** tell us that dragon blood
is like a magic medicine.

DID YOU KNOW?
In some places people believed dragons could control the rain.

The dragon myth

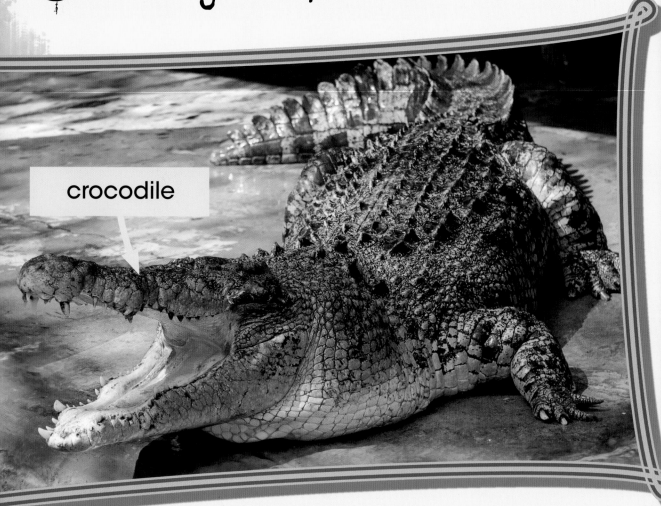

crocodile

Myths about dragons began thousands of years ago. There are stories about dragons in the **Bible**, Greek myths, and other old **legends**. Why did so many people believe in dragons?

Where did the dragon myth come from?

Did people think:

- lizards, alligators, crocodiles, or snakes were dragons?

- lightning in the sky was a dragon breathing fire?

- a volcano erupting was a dragon roaring?

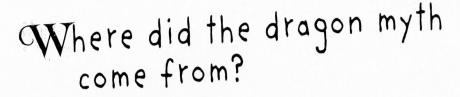

volcano

Dragons of China

Dragons have been important in China for thousands of years. Chinese people believed dragons could be friendly and would bring them good luck.

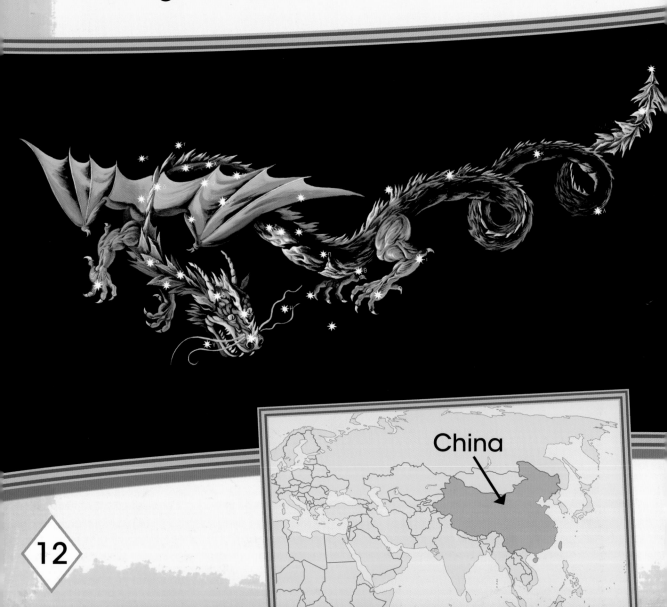

China

Every twelve years in China it is the Year of the Dragon. People born in this year are supposed to have good luck and a long life.

Chinese dragons weren't always helpful. Some stories tell us how dragons got angry when humans didn't **respect** them. Then they would stop the rain or bring floods.

DID YOU KNOW?
People in China did dragon dances and raced dragon boats to keep the dragons happy.

Dragons of Europe

Dragons in Europe were fierce monsters. Many people thought they were giant winged snakes living in underground caves. Many stories told of dragons burning down villages and taking young women away.

England

Wales

Europe

DID YOU KNOW?

People believed that dragons guarded treasure. **Knights** would try to kill a dragon and take its treasure.

17

Many famous **legends** tell of heroes fighting dragons. An old English poem is about the hero named Beowulf (say *bay-oh-wolf*) fighting a snake-like dragon. Another story tells us that Saint George killed a dragon and rescued a princess.

Saint George

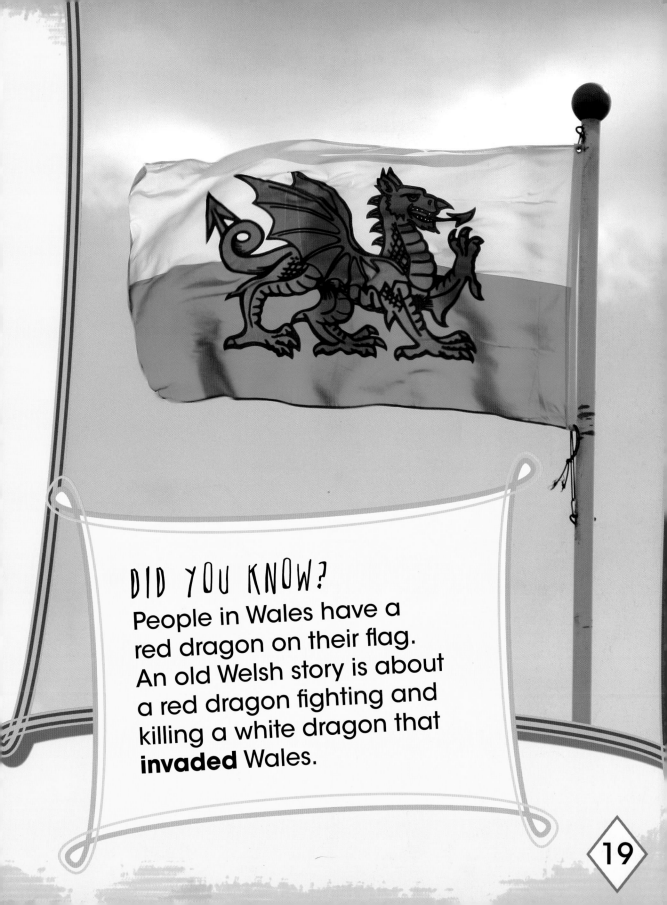

DID YOU KNOW?

People in Wales have a
red dragon on their flag.
An old Welsh story is about
a red dragon fighting and
killing a white dragon that
invaded Wales.

19

American dragons

People also tell dragon **myths** in North and South America. In Central America there is a myth about the dragon god Chac (say *chock*). He controlled the water so people gave him gifts for rain.

North America

Colombia

Central America

South America

In Colombia people believed in a goddess called Bachue (say *bash-oo-ey*). They thought she **created** humans and then turned herself and her husband into dragons.

This is a statue of another South American dragon goddess.

Dragons of the Middle East

In the Middle East, there are many stories about dragons. In Babylon people talked about a scaly dragon called the sirrush (say *ser-RUSH*). This dragon had back legs like an eagle. In Sumeria people believed in a snake-like dragon called Kur. Babylon and Sumeria were where Iraq is now.

ancient Sumerian temple

People believed the sirrush had a long neck and a horn on its head. It also had a forked tongue.

Middle East

Iraq

Close relatives

There are other creatures in **myths** that are similar to dragons. Myths from Europe tell about a reptile like a snake with two legs and wings called a wyvern (say *why-vurn*).

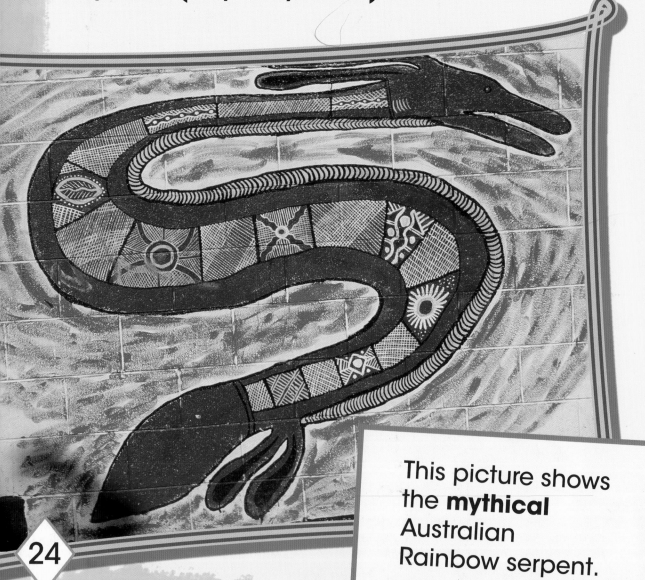

This picture shows the **mythical** Australian Rainbow serpent.

DID YOU KNOW?

Some people believed in a monster called a basilisk (say *bass-ill-isk*). A real basilisk is a lizard that can run across water!

Could dragons exist?

 They could be real...

- People all over the world tell stories about dragons.

 I'm not so sure...

- You can't believe all the stories you hear. Lots of stories around the world are similar.

 They could be real...

- Dragons could be hiding deep in mountain caves.

 I'm not so sure...

- Dragons are supposed to be so big that surely we would have seen one.

They could be real...

- We now know dinosaurs used to live on Earth. Maybe dragons did too.

 I'm not so sure...

- Scientists have found remains of dinosaurs. They haven't found any **evidence** of dragons.

There are many interesting stories about dragons. What do you think?

Reality versus myth

Komodo dragon (real)

Found: Indonesia

Lives: on hot, dry islands

Eats: birds, small animals, baby Komodo dragons

Seen: young Komodo dragons can hide in trees, older ones dig holes in the shade to rest

Special power: has a poisonous bite.

Dragon (myth)

Found: all over the world

Lives: deep in underground caves or in pools of water

Eats: people

Seen: in paintings and in films

Special power: magic.

Glossary

Bible special book in the Christian religion

create make something, or make something happen

evidence facts that tell us if something is true

invade attack

knight fighter from the past. Knights often wore armour and rode horses.

legend traditional story that may or may not be true

myth traditional story, often about magical creatures and events

mythical found in myths

respect treat someone politely and properly

Find out more

Books

Dragon Poems, John Foster and Korky Paul
(Oxford University Press, 2004)

Herb the Vegetarian Dragon, Jules Bass
(Barefoot Books, 2005)

The Usborne Book of Myths and Legends,
Gill Doherty (Usborne Publishing, 2006)

Working With Dragons, Helen Ward
(Templar Publishing, 2004)

Websites

http://pbskids.org/dragontales/index_sw.html
This website is full of games and activities that are
all about dragons!

**www.woodlands-junior.kent.sch.uk/customs/
stgeorge2.html**
Read all about the legend of Saint George and
the dragon.

Index